FIGURES OF THE HUMAN

FIGURES OF
THE HUMAN

Poems by DAVID IGNATOW

Wesleyan University Press, MIDDLETOWN, CONNECTICUT

Certain of the poems in this volume are reprinted from the author's earlier books, *Poems* (Decker Press, 1948) and *The Gentle Weight Lifter* (Morris Gallery, 1955). Others have previously appeared in the following periodicals, to which grateful acknowledgment is made: *Beloit Poetry Journal, Carleton Miscellany, Chelsea No. 12, The Nation, Quarterly Review of Literature, The Sixties,* and *Voices.* The poems "Beautiful and Kind," "If My Hand," and "To Nowhere" originally appeared in *Poetry.*

Library of Congress Catalog Card Number: 64-22373
Manufactured in the United States of America
FIRST EDITION

FOR ROSE GRAUBART

CONTENTS

FIGURES OF THE HUMAN

TO AN APPLE

You were rotten
and I sliced you into pieces
looking for a wholesome part,
then threw you into the street.
You were eaten by a horse,
dipping his head to nibble
gently at the skin.
I heard later he became violently ill,
died and was shipped off
to be processed. I think about it
and write of the good in you.

AND THAT NIGHT

A photo is taken of the family
enjoying the sunshine
and that night someone sneaks up
from behind in your flat
as you sit reading the papers
and clobbers you. You never
find out why or who, you just
lean back and die.
The sunshine is gone too,
the photograph gets into the news.
You bring up a family in three small rooms,
this crazy man comes along
to finish it off.

PLAY AGAIN

[Late in 1962 New York newspapers reported
the story of a nine-year-old child being raped on
a roof, and hurled twenty stories to the ground.]

I draw near to the roof's edge
and seek someone to lift
and hurl me out into vacant air.
I want to turn over and over
rapidly in my plunge, my mouth
open to scream but air rushing
upwards jams my throat.
I am seeking the peace
I never once gave up on
and this is the final way
to find it. The living
share me among them. They taste
me on the ground, they taste me
in the air descending. They taste
me screaming, nine years old.
I have playmates
and I leave behind my skull
in their dreams, hands to mouths.
It is because they have no help,
as if to hint to them the way,
if they would understand.
When we played it was to love each other
in games. Play again and love me
until I really die, when you are old
on a flight of stairs.

EMERGENCY CLINIC

Come in with your stab wound up the middle.
You say two cars collided, you caught
in between — and your breath stinks
of liquor. You were found staggering
under the Atlantic Avenue El
in the empty street outside a bar;
a figure escaping into the dark —
someone known to you, no doubt,
with whom leaning over a drink
you discussed white men
with jocular hatred. Is there no
comradeship in misery either?
Less drunk than you, therefore more desperate,
it was his turn to use the knife,
as it was yours no doubt, some night before
on the case now in the morgue,
or if not you then someone who could stand
in your place and will lie in your place
tomorrow. Do not bother to tell me
the truth, since you do presume I know
by your graceless dodge. You know comradeship
in our shared knowledge,
in the anger that I feel towards you
and towards myself.

TWO VOICES

I'll challenge myself, I said.
I have read the classics;
my insides feel they'd like to be outside
catching air. It was cold
but sunny. I wore my coat,
no hat though. Adventure.
I would invite trouble at once.
Pneumonia. I'll escape Stendhal,
Baudelaire, Whitman, Eliot,
each pressing me in turn
to his heart. In the cold air
I hardened. Nearby stood a lake;
I jumped in.
        "We had to haul him
out, a block of ice, eyeballs
in a frozen stare. After melting him
down, we lost him. He had forgotten
how to breathe. 'Challenge the weather,'
he murmured. 'Challenge the weather.'
And he closed his eyes."

TICK TOCK

Have you just stabbed a man to death? Live.
Are you a thief? Prosper.
Do you sell dope? Be well.
If there is no life, there is no murder,
no robbery, no dope peddling.
Stab, drink yourself blind,
go like a rocket, burst in the dark.
Come down in pieces, tick tock.

TO NOWHERE

I carry my keys like a weapon,
their points bunched together
and held outwards in the palm
for a step too close behind me
as I approach the subway through the dark.
Drunks are swaying against walls,
hopped-up men are leaning over
and dancing together crazily
and clapping hands, their faces twitching.
Quiet ones lounge against the wall watching.
They look for the weakness
in a man where they can jump him
and my keys are sure sign.
I walk as I always do, quickly,
my face set straight ahead
as I pretend not to see or hear,
busy on a mission to nowhere.

THE GAME

Hunt me down
and I will turn
to knife you in the groin.
Jump back
and I will jump to attack
and receive your counterblow
of the club. Back and forth
we'll step, excited,
panting,
joyful.

EARTH HARD

Earth hard to my heels
bear me up like a child
standing on its mother's belly.
I am a surprised guest to the air.

I AM WELL

For WCW

Say, what is it . . .
I have put a knife in the sun:
gleam of my self in transport —
knife of my dream: sacrificial
edge to see me through. I am
exposed to you, offered
by desires from the sea.
Fish me from the flood,
bring me shiny to shore,
my unsteady dream. Knife
that can bring solace, cut me
where I am not free. Rose
of my dying fill me,
I breathe for you,
I am awake,
I am well.

NAT KOFFMAN: 1910–1950

I did not know myself and painted
the alternating moods of hope and darkness,
as if to meld them into stillness.

Though I confronted people slowly
and laconically, it was a mask.
I could feel a presence, I had begun to sense
that this had to be painted —
my outward stillness.
I found canvas after canvas heavy with it —
when this happened; as if to point
at my theme.
        I am content, really;
I have my work to show.

I'LL COME BACK

I'll tear up the floor
outside my room,
I'll open my door
on a precipice,
I'll be compact,
I'll shout
and have an echo.

I'll be happy
when I can call myself
a fool in comfort,
I'll spring with the breaking sounds
powdered on the wind's path
like a veil carried to sea
to marry the fish.
I'll be no whale,
I'll be water,
I'll come back to shore.

THE YEARS OF LOSS

I love the beginning, always a promise.
I love the middle period
when all are committed
and I love the years of climax
when the beginning is possessed
in the face and the years of loss
in evidence.

IN A DREAM

Out of a crowd he steps
towards the iron gate
surrounding the fountain
and recites to himself
between the bars
two lines of a poem
newly arrived —
two lines that he repeats
again and again
until in that talkative crowd
several turn to stare
and say, It's his life he leads,
and look away.

FIGURES OF THE HUMAN

My love, pills in her purse,
runs, now staggering, now flushed,
her speech racing near the world:
whisper talk to it, dangling,
"Let creatures ride her, soften hard bumps
for them." Who warns her from self,
racing, singing, lightfooted?
Birds, dogs, cats screech, bark, mew,
conversant with air.
                        Raise her from swooning,
the childhood spirit. Catch her
skittering, mewing with joy, barking delirium.
Then are we loved, hand drawing swiftly
figures of the human struggling awake.

AND THE SAME WORDS

I like rust on a nail,
fog on a mountain.
Clouds hide stars,
rooms have doors,
eyes close,
and the same words
that began love
end it
with changed emphasis.

IF MY HAND

If my hand believes in death,
wielding a knife, my mind
relates it to the living
for love or its lack.
I have ordered it,
eating or sleeping,
and honor the routine,
each death affirmative.

I WAS ANGRY

I was angry,
drove you mad,
with peace to myself.
Being sane now,
I am shown your fear
which reads me
from its dark hiding.
You secretly survive.

I CAN BE SEEN

I can be seen each Sunday
carrying a handbag stuffed
with clothes and food for you.
So long as I live
I will be known for this.
If I have been cruel
then that was me,
gripping the handbag
as I stood waiting for you
to come out of your ward.
I'll be your father and disappear,
only knowing that you
are well again, dressed to leave
and combing your hair.

THE SKY IS BLUE

Put things in their place,
my mother shouts. I am looking
out the window, my plastic soldier
at my feet. The sky is blue
and empty. In it floats
the roof across the street.
What place, I ask her.

THE SONG

The song is to emptiness.
One may come and go
without a ripple. You see it
among fish in the sea,
in the woods among the silent
running animals, in a plane
overhead, gone; man
bowling or collecting coins,
writing about it.

BEAUTIFUL AND KIND

Outside my window
floats the head of a woman
looking in. Strangely,
I live on the top floor.
She reminds me of the one
in my dream — serene,
beautiful and kind,
in whom all said shines
with goodness on her face,
even as I denounce her a fraud.
I must kiss her, I say in gratitude,
and prepare to step out the window.

LAST NIGHT

Last night I spoke to a dead woman with green face.
She told me of her good life among the living,
with a faithful man. He was right there
beside her as tall as I, and moving
like me, with kind motions. If she did breathe,
it was just to talk and tell her life
in their basement smelling moist
like freshly opened earth. He was good to her
and she had worked as a typist
every day and came home to cook.
It was a good life with her husband,
he was kind; and she took hold of his hand
and said, "In this basement we've made a home,
with me working as typist and he studying
his music." She was dead, that much she understood
herself by her tone; and she looked at me
with green eyes.

PLAYFULLY

Lovely death of the horse
lying on its side, legs bent
as in gallop, and firm policeman
pointing his gun at the horse's head:
dull sound of the shot, twitch
along the body, the head
leaping up from the ground
and dropping —
to hold me by its death
among children
home from school, the sky calm.

Playfully, I note my grey head.

TWO FRIENDS

I have something to tell you.
I'm listening.
I'm dying.
I'm sorry to hear.
I'm growing old.
It's terrible.
It is, I thought you should know.
Of course and I'm sorry. Keep in touch.
I will and you too.
And let know what's new.
Certainly, though it can't be much.
And stay well.
And you too.
And go slow.
And you too.

NO THEORY

No theory will stand up to a chicken's guts
being cleaned out, a hand rammed up
to pull out the wriggling entrails,
the green bile and the bloody liver;
no theory that does not grow sick
at the odor escaping.

ON WALKING INTO A DARK ALLEY

Look into these shadows
I am promised to be caught in,
my hands merged with shadow,
my mind a phantasmal wall,
my past like a dark streamer behind me.
I will fade into the shadows
the purpose of which I trust
God knows.

THE PLANT

With one part rooted in resignation
by which the blooming part has strength,
it sends the sun down,
making the dark transient.

WALKING

I've got to have the things that hurt me.
People want to deprive me of them in pity.
It is they who are made miserable
by my painful life, and I am sorry
for them without weights upon their feet,
walking.

THE VENDING MACHINE

I look at a vending machine filled
with candies and say to it,
Disgorge yourself, one for me
and all the rest for the others.
But the machine remains stolid
and silent. It needs a nickel
to make it work, and I remain
stolid and silent.

FOR ONE MOMENT

You take the dollar
and hand it to the fellow beside you
who turns and gives it to the next one
down the line. The world being round,
you stand waiting, smoking and lifting
a cup of coffee to your lips, talking
of seasonal weather and hinting
at problems. The dollar returns,
the coffee spills to the ground
in your hurry. You have the money
in one hand, a cup in the other,
a cigarette in your mouth,
and for one moment have forgotten
what it is you have to do,
your hair grey, your legs weakened
from long standing.

ABOUT MONEY

The wonder of cherries
has gone into the wonder of money.
My mind is green with anxiety
about money.

THE NAILHEAD

"Keep the money coming in,"
hammers at me. At night
I run a hand over the job
and cannot find myself,
flush with it. I dig
at the surface to clear
an area around the nailhead.
My fingernails break,
I switch hands. I keep scraping
at myself emerging bit by bit,
weary beyond rest.
I need a sedative.
After a day driving myself
and then to spend the night
yanking needs someone insane
and I stand ready for tomorrow too.

TOMORROW

Whose the power, I ask,
you asleep, for decisions;
whom to trust; whose motives
are worthy, my child?
In whose shadow will we walk?
Who will give us to think?
We will resist in a manner
but to whom the power
and you asleep, baby,
your face of pink milk,
and I am rocking you asleep.

SIMULTANEOUSLY

Simultaneously, five thousand miles apart,
two telephone poles, shaking and roaring
and hissing gas, rose from their emplacements
straight up, leveled off and headed
for each other's land, alerted radar
and ground defense, passed each other
in midair, escorted by worried planes,
and plunged into each other's place,
steaming and silent and standing straight,
sprouting leaves.

STIEGLITZ

Stieglitz wore a cape to taunt bulls
in his china shop, and those who were offended
had it thrown at them, with a smile.
Stieglitz at eighty wore it every day,
as much as any time when he was young,
and lacked only the strength to throw hard,
as he did then, but said, almost politely,
"Why don't you leave, if you don't like it?"
And no one left. Because they were offended,
and had to learn.
        "Listen," he said one day,
lying on his couch in the back room. "Don't
excite me with new paintings at my age.
I'll take my stand on what I've found,
and let life be my ally for the future.
My pictures and my photographs will do something.
The way weakness hinders my own effort now
I am better dead. Then what I have done already
will be left to encourage others, whom I have no strength
to encourage now.
        "And goodbye, bull,
in my china shop. Come back a lamb.
Even sell your business, you big broker.
Anyway, don't paint.
At least, just think a moment this:
To whom are you dictating, when you dictate?
Who is listening, telling you what
it takes to be wise,
and you have nothing but facts.

They are thrown into fire
and the fool snatches at the blaze.
Says the broker, 'Let him do it,
I won't.' And does nothing
and looks it."
                    Stieglitz, all ideas
came to one for you, lucky man.
You believed in and said, "Start
from any point and come towards the thorny bush,
where Moses saw a God blaze. Let us
all see what we can, but with the heart in it.
All must be malleable in flame —
marble or stone or rock.
To the stake with all of you,
be light for the time you live."

NURSE

The old man who can undress before you
as easily as before a mirror believes
that you are only the matured concept of his body,
as idea only.
        Let us hope your uniform
does not deceive him, in that you are dedicated
to his care. The dress you wear is white
for the abolition of all your woes before his;
for he has worn the body of his time
a little longer and a little more indulgently
than you, whose cries of welcome or goodbye
beneath his window on your night leave
will wake him fitfully from the dream
of the burden of earth given back to earth again.

You are to know that body is love
of having been born, and to grow old
is to be born into returning to the good
from which we come. You have eyes
to see no shame but resignation
in his stooped figure,
such as love brings.
        And now, your own eyes
are colorless of wrong,
and each look is to follow
one man's devotion to growing old.
You take his clothes from him,
and let him rest;
and in your going to and fro
from cabinet to cot carry instruments
of your respect to his side,
in tribute to him.

PARK

I sit beside old retired Italians.
They chat, and have smooth skins.
Their hair is white, and the flesh full.
They make no disturbance.
They rest all day, sitting in a park.
One will come over from his house
and add to the crowd.
      They never
grow loud. They talk and laugh,
solid company every day. I love
to come here and sit with them,
I a stranger, and feel the quiet
and stability they make,
and lasting custom.

GET THE GASWORKS

Get the gasworks into a poem,
and you've got the smoke and smokestacks,
the mottled red and yellow tenements,
and grimy kids who curse with the pungency
of the odor of gas. You've got America, boy.

Sketch in the river and barges,
all dirty and slimy.
How do the seagulls stay so white?
And always cawing like little mad geniuses?
You've got the kind of living
that makes the kind of thinking we do:
gaswork smokestack whistle tooting wisecracks.
They don't come because we like it that way,
but because we find it outside our window each morning,
in soot on the furniture,
and trucks carrying coal for gas,
the kid hot after the ball under the wheel.
He gets it over the belly, all right.
He dies there.

So the kids keep tossing the ball around
after the funeral.
So the cops keep chasing them,
so the mamas keep hollering,
and papa flings his newspaper outward,
in disgust with discipline.

BOWERY

Bums ask themselves, Why dress and shave,
and be well mannered, studious and hard-working,
abstain from liquor and raise children,
own home and debts, a bank account and business friends,
when others more eager are doing it successfully?
All we want is the luxury of our failures,
the right to sit propped up against a wall,
drunk and drooling, letting urine seep
through our clothes onto the sidewalk,
we unconscious or unconcerned.
Our failures show us to our victories,
at each succeeding degradation we find employment
in forgetfulness.
         None among you wealthy or hard-working
can say as much, though with money to afford it.
We with none relax anyway, letting the world
come in on us in sidewalk spit on which we sprawl,
in kicks and jabs from cops, under open skies
in rain and snow. None of you who can
dare do it, and so you do not know what money means.
We who live on charity enjoy the pleasure
of your wealth, the smoke-filled air,
the raucous nights, the long hours filled with drunkenness.

EUROPE AND AMERICA

My father brought the emigrant bundle
of desperation and worn threads,
that in anxiety as he stumbles
tumble out distractedly;
while I am bedded upon soft green money
that grows like grass. Thus,
between my father who lives on a bed of anguish
for his daily bread, and I who tear money
at leisure by the roots,
where I lie in sun or shade,
a vast continent of breezes, storms to him,
shadows, darkness to him, small lakes,
difficult channels to him, and hills,
mountains to him, lie between us.

My father comes of a hell
where bread and man have been kneaded
and baked together. You have heard the scream
as the knife fell; while I have slept
as guns pounded on the shore.

REFLECTION BESIDE A LAKE

In a quiet moment we pause
to contemplate the things that make us discontent.
If all is still a moment longer
than we had expected, we want to believe
that this is it. This is what
we have been looking for in life.
Here is its goodness. This is life
at last as we had expected it to be.
We make fools of ourselves with speeches
and optimism, and go forth out
of our quiet cells to be upset again,
and to curse life.
                    The peace and silence
of the lake are fooling me too,
making me believe that life is sweet.
Don't you know that it is only a pause?
Out of sourness you must make your bread.
Your trouble shall become sweet with use,
and all bitterness will turn into a theme
for love.

BROODING

The sadness of our lives.
We will never be good enough to each other,
to our parents and friends.
We go along like old sailing ships,
loaded with food and drink for a long voyage,
self-sufficient, without any outside contact
with the world.
               The truth faces me
all the time. We are in a world
in which nobody listens to anybody,
in which we do as we please
until we are stopped by others.
We live our whole lives as in a husk,
which keeps us separate from any influence.
While those who reflect the influence
of others are either idiots, or people
who never gained consciousness.

A GUIDED TOUR THROUGH THE ZOO

Ladies and gentlemen,
these are pygmies, fated to live
in small perspective: children
of their shrunk parents, who
because of stubborn pride fed
on small seeds and herbs, scrabbled
together with hooded eyes; and so
were grown to such likeness. But
in turn had been shut in by their parents
in caves to be told night was day;
for their parents' parents were fledged
on the precipice from which they fled
to these caves, and so on, giving us
this tribe before us.
                 The story is sad,
for they remember by lost meanings
of words that they were of Hercules,
who could move earth for fleas to rest
easy, or sheep to roll softly downhill.
They were men, so called, in their unworded
language, which, when the sun grows brutal
with them as with rocks, they cry
remembrance in these open fields,
their homes under the short grass.
Ladies and gentlemen, let us move on
now to the cage of wild wolves.

IN ANCIENT TIMES

And they took Abu and stoked the fire with him,
and then Azu, after Abu was consumed,
to keep the blaze high. It was a night
of wild animals, a fire was needed to ward them off.
Abu by his own choice was killed for fuel
and then Azu to keep the others safe;
and so on down the line, one by one,
until morning. Men, women and children
who would not die in this manner
were forced to by their own hand,
for the sake of the others,
after a long talk.

And in the morning
the great band arose from around the dead ash
and moved on to new grounds and new possibilities;
and in the afternoon as always
when they were starved paired off
and killed each other for their food.
There was nothing to eat over the whole
wide plain of their wandering, and nothing
to work with to turn the soil —
like lead, anyhow. They had come
by a blind route from orchards and fields
in their wandering to this forsakenness,
over which the lions howled
for the flesh that crawled by.

PROMENADE

His head split in four parts,
he walks down the street — pleasant
with shady trees and a sun softened
by leaves touching it. He walks,
a revolving turret for a head,
from each slit of which he looks guardedly:
the enemy approaches or he approaches
the enemy. At any moment the chatter of differences
will break out; the four parts of his skull
revolve slowly, seeking the time.

In there they do not know of each other,
sealed off by steel walls. They are safer
together, singly and apart; and shouting,
angry or in pain, have only themselves
to listen; while overhead, ignored in the walk,
are the leaves, touching each other and the sun.

MOVING PICTURE

When two take gas
by mutual consent
and the cops come in
when the doors are broken down
and the doctor pays respect
by closing the books
and the neighbors stand about
sniffing and afraid
and the papers run a brief
under a whiskey ad
and the news is read
eating ice cream or a fruit
and the paper is used
to wrap peelings
and the garbage man
dumps the barrel
into the truck
and the paper flares
in the furnace and sinks back
charred and is scooped up
for mud flats and pressed down
by steam rollers for hard ground
and a house on it
for two to enter.

THE SPHINX

[On holidays the Egyptians together with their
children play an obstacle-racing game on these
stones.]

They had stood in the sun and piled up these stones
to tell us life was that hard and that high and wide
and filled with so many tall steps that needed our hands
and legs and full strength to rise upon; and now
descendants, lives no grander, no gayer, no easier
by one less stone — who still drink from sandy wells,
they do not deny it — clamber upon them
with their children on a picnic spree.

What have you taught them
but the exercise of their wills,
to make a jest of their hardships?

They shall ascend, each child and his parent,
to wisdom's face and mount the body
as on a flying lion for the love of it
that one moment permits before the next;
and then, not to fall to tears and helpless rage,
descend racing in a game.

THE SALESMAN

What a busy man I was, I had first to step into one place
to confirm a price, and then on to the next to fix a date
and in that same building visit a third. There was even
more in those two hours but I hurried with legs stretched
out ahead of me like a horse and when through, exhausted,
plopped into a seat in a courtroom near my last errand
where the listening was free, and heard three men
condemned to prison for larceny, felony and assault
respectively, and each one take it calmly
and each as normal as myself in looks;
they stood quiet before the judge;
and then two women for assault upon their neighbors —
given each three months. But only one difference
did I note: I wore a business suit —
and I did think they spoke ungrammatically,
with no feeling. In effect
they said nothing before the judge,
and I sitting there noticing the courtroom crowded
with such cases, badged men strolling among them
to keep order, and men along the walls to overlook
the room, and hour after hour going by and no letup,
the court crowded as ever; they were, literally,
being brought in off the streets. I left
and went out into traffic.

SALES TALK

Better than to kill each other off
with our extra energy is to run after the bus,
though another be right behind. To run
and to explain to ourselves we have no time
to waste, when it is time that hangs
dangerously on our hands, so that the faster
we run the quicker the breezes rushing by
take time away.
         For comfort we must work
this way, because in the end we find
fume-filled streets and murder headlines:
one out of insanity breaks loose:
he could not make that extra effort
to keep connected with us. Loneliness
like a wheeling condor was attracted
to the particle that had strayed apart.

The brief case we carry, the pressed trousers,
the knotted tie under a white collar, add up
to unity and morale.

THE BUSINESS LIFE

When someone hangs up, having said
to you, "Don't come around again,"
and you have never heard the phone
banged down with such violence
nor the voice vibrate with such venom,
pick up your receiver gently and dial
again, get the same reply; and dial
again, until he threatens. You will
then get used to it, be sick only
instead of shocked. You will live,
and have a pattern to go by, familiar
to your ear, your senses and your dignity.

THE AMERICAN

And they come begging for money
with scorn, proud of their own past
where money had no part. They had fought
battles and died brave, dedicated
to love or to philosophy. He must bow
his head in deference and give.
They have not asked him how his wealth
was made, in what self-doubt and aspiration,
emptiness there. To make something solid
out of air, the thick woods and tough hills
that repelled him. He had dug, cursing
and brawling to keep up his grit,
and grew coarse to keep the strength strong;
for he had inherited a vast emptiness
of wild animals and grass of which
he could not eat steadily without turning.
Before him stood this dim past,
a ghost to drive him, terrified
by its glory, to escape and make a present
equal to it and unafraid.
He has it in his wealth.

I WANT

I'll tell him I want to be paid immediately.
I'll sue him, I'll tear down his place,
I'll throw a fit, I'll show him whether
he can make me miserable.
I want things perfect.
I want to know I can expect a check
tomorrow morning at nine o'clock
exactly, with the mailman,
and if he doesn't bring it
I'll know that he too has done it
on purpose. He too knows
I have a family and a business
that are going to be made miserable by me.
At home I'll snarl and in the office
nobody will talk to me,
I'll talk to nobody,
and over the phone I'll whine
about money. Is that nice?
And what will people think of me?
It'll be some world,
a horrible one already,
the way I'm upset and with nothing to do
but rave, rave, rave.
I want my check!

THE MEN SANG

Nicias warned them: in Sicily stood ruin;
in no country were they wanted,
in their own they were besieged.
What could Athenians seek to gain?
And Athens roared back, Traitor!
And Alcibiades got secretly together
his compatriots to desecrate the state,
to hasten their rupture with the past —
of freedom and forbearance; Nicias
made to take command of all forces,
challenged to. Gold glittered in their eyes,
from Syracuse. And against every impulse,
sick with grief, foreboding each step,
Nicias set sail; and the men sang,
and rowed as never before.

OEDIPUS

My hands shook as I bargained for passage,
my hands shook because by his face I could tell
he was not one I could bargain with; death only
was his price. And when he lashed out at me
from his pre-eminence, his chariot, my hand
leapt to my sword, my throat ached.
I had no head then to consider I was killing
one who like myself had not been brought up
to countenance such manners, as to bargain.
Only against my grain I had wanted to.
I killed him, I felt myself cut off;
I heard myself inwardly go mad,
I had destroyed an image I hated:
I was destroyed.

BOTHERING ME AT LAST

Where is my mother?
Has she gone to the store for food,
or is she in the cellar shoveling coal
into the furnace to keep the house warm?
Or is she on her knees scrubbing the floor?
I thought I saw her in bed
holding a hand to her heart, her mouth open:
"I can't breathe, son. Take me to a hospital."
I looked for her in the cellar.
I looked for her in bed, and found her in her coffin,
bothering me at last.

DILEMMA

Whatever we do, whether we light
strangers' cigarettes — it may turn out
to be a detective wanting to know who is free
with a light on a lonely street nights —
or whether we turn away and get a knife
planted between our shoulders for our discourtesy;
whatever we do — whether we marry for love
and wake up to find love is a task,
or whether for convenience to find love
must be won over, or we are desperate —
whatever we do; save by dying,
and there too we are caught,
by being planted too close to our parents.

FOR ALL FRIENDS

Talking together, we advance from loneliness
to where words fall off into space
and send up no echo. Looking down
for instruction, we gaze into the crease
and fold of each other's face.
We are falling from the precipice of heaven,
our flesh aged by life's upward force.
Our words are buried in the falling air.
Deep in the ground, with time's impact,
we will be one with our words,
for earth too falls towards eternity.

MYSTIQUE

No man has seen the third hand
that stems from the center, near the heart.
Let either the right or left prepare
a dish for the mouth, or a thing
to give, and the third hand deftly
and unseen will enter to change the object
of our hunger or of our giving.

THE DEBATE

This man brings me stones
out of the ground. These
are eggs, he says, of the Jurassic
age, hardened. They may
be looked upon as eggs.
And taking them in awe
I drop them. They bounce,
one strikes me on the toe,
I wince. They are eggs,
he repeats calmly.
They are stones, I shout.
Stone, stone! They were eggs
in their day and bruise me now.
They are eggs, ossified,
he amends calmly.
And I will not let you
fry them for breakfast,
I answer sweetly,
because they are stone.

NEWS REPORT

At two A.M. a thing, jumping out of a manhole,
the cover flying, raced down the street,
emitting wild shrieks of merriment and lust.
Women on their way from work, chorus girls
or actresses, were accosted with huge leers
and made to run; all either brought down
from behind by its flying weight, whereat
it attacked blindly, or leaping ahead,
made them stop and lie down.
Each, hysterical, has described it in her way,
one giving the shaggy fur, the next the shank bone
of a beast, and a third its nature
from which, as it seemed, pus dribbled,
when she saw no more —
                                        all taking place
unnoticed until the first report, hours later
when consciousness was regained, and each
from diverse parts of the city has a tell-tale
sign, the red teeth marks sunk into the thigh
and the smell of a goat clinging tenaciously
through perfume and a bath.

THE WESLEYAN POETRY PROGRAM

Distinguished books of contemporary poetry
available in cloth-bound and paperback editions
published by Wesleyan University Press

Alan Ansen:	*Disorderly Houses* (1961)
John Ashbery:	*The Tennis Court Oath* (1962)
Robert Bagg:	*Madonna of the Cello* (1961)
Robert Bly:	*Silence in the Snowy Fields* (1962)
Donald Davie:	*New and Selected Poems* (1961)
James Dickey:	*Drowning With Others* (1962)
James Dickey:	*Helmets* (1964)
David Ferry:	*On the Way to the Island* (1960)
Robert Francis:	*The Orb Weaver* (1960)
Richard Howard:	*Quantities* (1962)
Barbara Howes:	*Light and Dark* (1959)
David Ignatow:	*Figures of the Human* (1964)
David Ignatow:	*Say Pardon* (1961)
Donald Justice:	*The Summer Anniversaries* (1960) (A Lamont Poetry Selection)
Chester Kallman:	*Absent and Present* (1963)
Vassar Miller:	*My Bones Being Wiser* (1963)
Vassar Miller:	*Wage War on Silence* (1960)
Donald Petersen:	*The Spectral Boy* (1964)
Hyam Plutzik:	*Apples from Shinar* (1959)
Vern Rutsala:	*The Window* (1964)
Louis Simpson:	*At the End of the Open Road* (1963) (Pulitzer Prize in Poetry, 1964)
Louis Simpson:	*A Dream of Governors* (1959)
James Wright:	*The Branch Will Not Break* (1963)
James Wright:	*Saint Judas* (1959)